Japan

Julie McCulloch

www.heinemann.co.uk
Visit our website to find out more information about **Heinemann Library** books.

To order:
☎ Phone 44 (0) 1865 888066
▤ Send a fax to 44 (0) 1865 314091
▢ Visit the Heinemann Bookshop at www.heinemann.co.uk to browse our catalogue and order online.

First published in Great Britain by Heinemann Library, Halley Court, Jordan Hill, Oxford OX2 8EJ, a division of Reed Educational and Professional Publishing Ltd. Heinemann is a registered trademark of Reed Educational & Professional Publishing Limited.

OXFORD MELBOURNE AUCKLAND JOHANNESBURG BLANTYRE
GABORONE IBADAN PORTSMOUTH NH (USA) CHICAGO

© Reed Educational and Professional Publishing Ltd 2002
The moral right of the proprietor has been asserted.

Designed by Tinstar Design (www.tinstar.co.uk)
Illustrations by Nicholas Beresford-Davies
Originated by Dot Gradations
Printed by Wing King Tong in Hong Kong

ISBN 0 431 11701 2   (hardback)
06 05 04 03 02
10 9 8 7 6 5 4 3 2

ISBN 0 431 11708 X   (paperback)
06 05 04 03 02
10 9 8 7 6 5 4 3 2 1

British Library Cataloguing in Publication Data
McCulloch, Julie
  Japan. – (A world of recipes)
  1. Cookery, Japanese – Juvenile literature 2.Japan –
  Description and travel – Juvenile literature
  I. Title
  641.5'123'0952

Acknowledgements
The Publishers would like to thank the following for permission to reproduce photographs:
Robert Harding, p.5. All other photographs: Gareth Boden.
Illustration: p.45, US Department of Agriculture/US Department of Health and Human Services.

Cover photographs reproduced with permission of Gareth Boden.

Our thanks to Sue Townsend, home economist, and Sue Mildenhall for their comments in the preparation of this book.

Every effort has been made to contact copyright holders of any material reproduced in this book. Any omissions will be rectified in subsequent printings if notice is given to the Publisher.

Words appearing in the text in bold, **like this**, are explained in the glossary.

Contents

Key

* easy

** medium

*** difficult

Japanese food

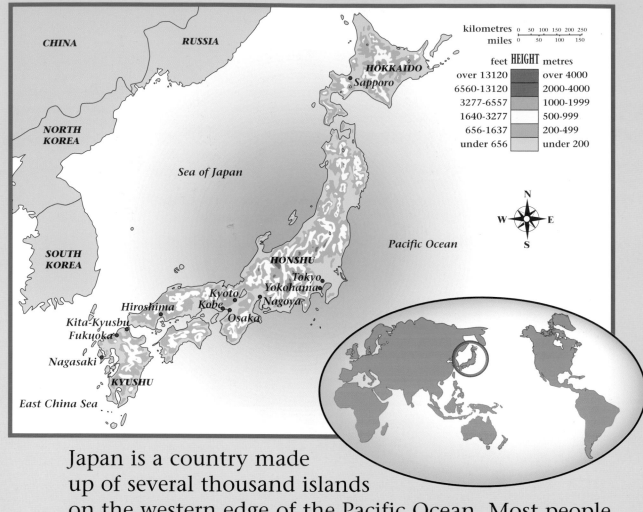

Japan is a country made up of several thousand islands on the western edge of the Pacific Ocean. Most people live on the largest island, called Honshu.

Japanese meals usually consist of rice, with lots of small dishes to accompany it. Food is cooked very simply and lightly, so that the taste of the natural ingredients comes through. Japanese people think that the way a dish looks is just as important as how it tastes.

In the past

Stone Age people settled in Japan more than 10,000 years ago. They lived by hunting, gathering and fishing. From 660 BC, Japan was ruled by emperors. In AD 1160, power passed to warriors called shoguns, who banned most people from contact with the rest of the world.

This **isolation** meant no outside influences affected Japanese food.

By the end of the nineteenth century, Japan became more open, and began to adopt some European and American ideas. After World War Two ended in 1945, Western influences started to affect Japanese cooking.

▲ *Many Japanese people buy fresh food every day from stalls like these.*

Around the country

The centre of Japan is mountainous. Most people live in the flatter areas around the coast. Japan's climate varies widely from north to south. In the north, winters are cold and snowy and summers are short. In the south the climate is hot and **humid**.

Different crops are grown in different areas of Japan, but the main crop is rice. Other crops include barley, soya beans, sweet potatoes, tea and citrus fruits. There are different food specialities around the country, too. Because most people in Japan live near the sea, fresh fish, seafood and seaweed are eaten everywhere.

Japanese meals

Traditionally, Japanese people don't have different foods for breakfast, lunch and dinner. Nearly every meal includes soup and rice, and perhaps three or four small vegetable, fish or meat dishes. Desserts are rare.

Japanese food is eaten with chopsticks. Food is often cut up into bite-sized pieces so that it can easily be picked up. See page 23 for how to use chopsticks.

Ingredients

Japanese cooking uses lots of ingredients which may be difficult to find outside Japan. You will find some in supermarkets, and some in oriental or health food shops. This book suggests alternatives for ingredients you may find hard to buy.

egg noodles

soy sauce

rice

sesame seeds

tofu

udon noodles

ginger

soba noodles

Dashi

'Dashi' is a liquid made from dried fish and seaweed. It is used in many dishes, but is difficult to find outside Japan. In this book we suggest using vegetable stock instead.

Ginger

Fresh ginger is used in many Japanese dishes, usually **peeled** and **grated**. It is readily available in supermarkets. It is better to use fresh rather than dried ginger, as it has more flavour.

Noodles

Noodles are very popular in Japan. There are many different types, but two of the most common types are 'soba' (thin brown noodles) and 'udon' (thick white noodles). These noodles are sometimes sold in supermarkets, but if you cannot get hold of them, use Chinese egg noodles, which are more widely available.

Rice

Rice is served at nearly every Japanese meal. Rice comes in two main types – short and long grain. Short grain rice is closer to the type of rice used in Japan.

Seaweed

Seaweed is used in many Japanese dishes. There are many different types. Three of the most common are 'nori' (black seaweed which is dried into sheets and used to wrap around rice, fish and vegetables), 'kombu' (dark green seaweed), and 'wakame' (dark green seaweed which is used in soups and salads). Seaweed is not an essential ingredient in this book.

nori seaweed

Sesame seeds

Sesame seeds are used to flavour many different Japanese dishes. **Toasting** them brings out their full flavour.

Soy sauce

This is one of the most important ingredients in Japanese cooking, and is used in nearly every dish. Soy sauce is called 'shoyu' in Japanese, and is made from soya beans, wheat, salt and water.

Tofu

Also called bean curd, tofu is made from **pulped** soya beans. It can be found in most supermarkets.

Before you start

Kitchen rules

There are a few basic rules you should always follow when you are cooking.

- Ask an adult if you can use the kitchen.
- Some cooking processes, especially those involving hot water or oil, can be dangerous. When you see this sign, take extra care or ask an adult to help.
- Wash your hands before you start.
- Wear an apron to protect your clothes, and tie back long hair.
- Be very careful when using sharp knives.
- Never leave pan handles sticking out in case you knock them.
- Always wear oven gloves to lift things in and out of the oven.
- Wash fruit and vegetables before you use them.

How long will it take?

Some of the recipes in this book are quick and easy, and some are more difficult and take longer. The strip across the top of the right hand page of each recipe tells you how long it will take to cook each dish from start to finish. It also shows how difficult each dish is to make: every recipe is either * (easy), ** (medium) or *** (difficult).

Quantities and measurements

You can see how many people each recipe will serve at the top of the right hand page, too. Most of the recipes in this book make enough to feed two people. Where it is sensible to make a larger amount, though, the recipe makes enough for four. You can multiply or divide the quantities if you want to cook for more or fewer people.

Ingredients for recipes can be measured in two ways. Metric measurements use grams and millilitres. Imperial measurements use ounces and fluid ounces. This book uses metric measurements. If you want to convert these into imperial measurements, see the chart on page 44.

In the recipes you will see the following abbreviations:

tbsp = tablespoon   g = grams
tsp = teaspoon   ml = millilitres

Utensils

To cook the recipes in this book, you will need these utensils (as well as kitchen essentials such as spoons, plates and bowls):

- chopping board
- chopsticks
- foil
- frying pan
- grater
- large, flat, ovenproof dish
- measuring jug
- metal or wooden skewers
- plastic lunch box
- roasting tin
- saucepan with lid
- set of scales
- sharp knife
- sieve or colander
- small ramekin dishes
- steamer (optional)

⓵ Whenever you use kitchen knives, be very careful.

9

Clear soup

Many Japanese people eat a bowl of soup for breakfast, or at the beginning of a formal meal. It is not eaten with a spoon – the idea is to pick out the solid ingredients with chopsticks, then pick up the bowl and drink the liquid.

What you need

½ carrot
1 spring onion
100g tofu
50g udon noodles (or Chinese egg noodles)
1 vegetable stock cube
2 tbsp soy sauce
½ tbsp granulated sugar

What you do

1 **Peel** the carrot, and cut it into thin **slices**.

2 Cut the top and bottom off the spring onion, and finely **chop** it.

3 Cut the tofu into small pieces, about ½ cm across.

4 Put 300ml water into a saucepan, and bring it to the **boil**. Slowly lower the noodles into the water. Turn the heat down, and leave the noodles to **simmer** for 4 minutes, until they are soft.

(!) 5 **Drain** the water from the noodles using a colander. Put them into the bottom of two small bowls.

6 Put 500ml water into a saucepan, and bring it to the boil. Crumble the stock cube into the water, and stir until it **dissolves**. Turn the heat down to a simmer.

7 Add the sliced carrot, chopped spring onion, tofu pieces, soy sauce and sugar to the stock.

8 Simmer the stock for 5 minutes.

9 Carefully pour the stock over the noodles, and serve.

ADDED EXTRAS

You can add many different ingredients to clear soup. Try adding a small amount of the following:

- sliced mushrooms
- spinach
- mangetout
- prawns

You can also add wakame seaweed to clear soup, if you can find some. You need to stand the wakame in cold water for about 20 minutes, until it is soft. Then cut it into strips about 1cm wide, and put it in the bottom of the bowl with the noodles.

Savoury custard

This savoury custard is a bit like a thick soup, and is called 'chawan mushi' in Japanese. It might be served at the end of a meal, or as a snack. It is usually eaten hot, but is sometimes served cold during the hot summer months.

What you need

1 vegetable stock cube
¼ tbsp granulated sugar
½ tbsp soy sauce
2 eggs

What you do

1 Put 225ml water into a saucepan, and bring it to the **boil**. Crumble the stock cube into the water, and stir until it **dissolves**. Turn the heat down to a **simmer**.

2 Add the sugar and soy sauce to the stock. Stir until the sugar dissolves.

3 Leave the stock to **cool** for about 15 minutes.

4 While the stock is cooling, crack the eggs into a bowl. **Beat** them with a fork or a whisk until the yolk and the white are mixed.

5 Pour the beaten eggs into the cooled stock, stirring gently as you pour.

6 Carefully pour the custard into two ramekin dishes.

7 Put the ramekin dishes in a steamer. Place the steamer over a pan of boiling water.

8 Turn the heat down to low. Put the lid on the steamer. **Steam** the custards for 30 minutes, until the mixture is set.

(!) 9 Wear an oven glove to remove the hot ramekins from the steamer. Serve your custards in these dishes.

COOKING IN THE OVEN

If you don't have a steamer, you can cook your custards in the oven. **Preheat** the oven to 220°C/425°F/gas mark 7. Half-fill a roasting tin with hot water, and place the ramekins full of custard in the water. **Cover** the whole roasting tin with foil. Put the tin in the oven, and cook the custards for 30 minutes.

TRY HUNTING!

Try adding other ingredients, such as mushrooms or prawns, to the basic custard, at stage 5. You can hunt for the different ingredients when you eat the custard!

Grilled tofu

The main religion in Japan is Buddhism. Buddhist temples often contain small restaurants, serving **vegetarian** food. Many of these dishes are based on tofu. This grilled tofu dish is typical of the sort of food served in temples. You could serve it as a starter or a snack.

What you need

150g tofu
1 tbsp soy sauce
1 tbsp granulated
   sugar
1 tbsp lemon juice
1 tbsp sesame seeds

What you do

1 Cut the tofu into 8 pieces, about 1cm thick.

2 Put the soy sauce, sugar and lemon juice into a bowl. Add the tofu pieces, and leave them to **marinate** for about an hour.

3 While the tofu is marinating, put the sesame seeds into a frying pan without adding any oil. Heat the seeds over a medium heat for about 5 minutes, keeping the pan moving, until they are golden brown. Some may pop out, so stand back! Put the **toasted** sesame seeds to one side.

4 When the tofu pieces are marinated, thread them onto skewers. If using wooden ones, soak them first.

5 Turn the grill on to a medium heat. **Grill** the tofu pieces on their skewers for 3 minutes on each side, until they are a golden brown colour, and cooked through.

6 Sprinkle the toasted sesame seeds over the tofu. Wait for the skewers to **cool** a little. Serve with a little dish of soy sauce to dunk the tofu in. Keep the tofu on the skewers, and nibble it off!

LOLLY STICKS

If you don't have skewers, you can grill the tofu on wooden 'lolly sticks', which you can buy from most supermarkets. Soak the lolly sticks in water for 10 minutes before using them so they will not burn under the grill.

15

Grilled chicken

This grilled chicken dish is called 'yakitori' in Japanese. Yakitori bars – small restaurants which only serve this dish – are found all over Japan.

What you need

2 chicken breasts
2 tbsp soy sauce
½ tbsp granulated sugar

What you do

1 Cut the chicken breasts into 2cm cubes.

2 Mix the soy sauce and sugar in a large, flat dish, and put the chicken pieces into the sauce. **Marinate** the chicken in the sauce for about an hour.

3 Thread the chicken pieces on to skewers. (If using wooden skewers, soak them first.)

4 Turn the grill on to a medium heat. **Grill** the marinated chicken pieces on their skewers for about 15 minutes. Halfway through, remove them from the grill. Wearing an oven glove, turn them and grill until golden brown and cooked through.

VEGETARIAN SKEWERS

You could use vegetables instead of, or as well as, chicken in this dish. Try pieces of courgette, mushroom or red pepper as shown in the photo below. You could cook them outside on a barbecue in the summer.

Chicken soup

This soup is served as a main course in Japan. As with clear soup on page 10, you eat the solid ingredients with chopsticks, then drink the liquid from the bowl.

What you need

250g udon noodles (or Chinese egg noodles)
1 vegetable stock cube
2 tbsp soy sauce
2 tbsp granulated sugar
2 chicken breasts
4 spring onions

What you do

1 Mix the soy sauce and sugar in a large, flat bowl.

2 Put the chicken breasts into the soy sauce and sugar mixture. Turn them over a couple of times until they are coated. Leave the chicken to **marinate** in the sauce for about an hour.

3 When the chicken has marinated, turn the grill on to a medium heat. **Grill** the marinated chicken for about 15 minutes, turning halfway through, until it is golden brown and cooked through.

(!) 4 Using a fork to lift it, carefully take the chicken out of the grill. Cut it into **slices**, using a sharp knife. Put them to one side.

5 Put 600ml water into a saucepan, and bring it to the **boil**. Crumble the stock cube into the water, and stir until it **dissolves**.

6 Add the noodles to the hot stock. Boil them for about 5 minutes, until they are soft.

7 Cut the tops and bottoms off the spring onions, and finely **chop** them.

⊘8 Pour the noodles and stock into two bowls. Arrange the chicken slices and the chopped spring onions on top of the noodles, then serve the soup.

Prawn and vegetable stir-fry

Food that is stirred while it is being fried over a high heat makes a dish called a **stir-fry**. The ingredients in this traditional stir-fry are cooked very quickly, so the vegetables should still taste crunchy.

What you need

½ courgette
60g mushrooms
2 spring onions
½ tbsp sunflower oil
150g prawns
100g bean sprouts
½ tbsp lemon juice
1 tbsp soy sauce

What you do

1 Cut the courgette and the mushrooms into **slices**.

2 Cut the tops and bottoms off the spring onions, and finely **chop** them.

(!) 3 Heat the oil in a frying pan.

4 Put the sliced courgette and mushrooms, prawns and bean sprouts into the frying pan. **Fry** the ingredients on a high heat, stirring continuously, for about 5 minutes.

5 Add the chopped spring onion, lemon juice and soy sauce to the frying pan, and cook for another 2 minutes before serving.

MORE STIR-FRY IDEAS

You could adapt this recipe to use all sorts of different ingredients. Try replacing the mushrooms and courgette with other vegetables, such as:

- sliced carrots
- sliced mushrooms
- mangetout
- pieces of broccoli

Chilled noodles

In parts of Japan where summers are very hot, noodles are sometimes served cold. Dip each mouthful of noodles into the sauce before you eat it.

What you need

1 spring onion
1 vegetable stock cube
50ml soy sauce
1 tbsp granulated sugar
100g soba noodles (or Chinese egg noodles)

What you do

1 Cut the top and bottom off the spring onion, and finely **chop** it.

2 Put 150ml water into a saucepan, and bring it to the **boil**. Crumble the stock cube into the water, and stir until it **dissolves**.

3 Add the soy sauce, sugar and chopped spring onion to the stock. **Simmer** the sauce for a couple of minutes until the sugar has dissolved.

4 Carefully pour the sauce into two small dishes, and leave to **cool**.

5 Put 300ml water into a pan and bring it to the boil.

6 Add the noodles, and cook them for about 5 minutes, until they are soft.

⚠ 7 Tip the noodles and hot water into a colander. Rinse the noodles in cold water, then **drain** them and put them into two small dishes.

8 Give each person a dish of noodles and a dish of sauce.

HOW TO USE CHOPSTICKS

Pick up one chopstick, and hold it between your thumb and first two fingers. This chopstick is the one that will move.

Put the second chopstick between your second and third fingers, and behind your thumb. This chopstick stays still. Move the top chopstick up and down with your thumb and first finger so that the tips of the chopsticks meet.

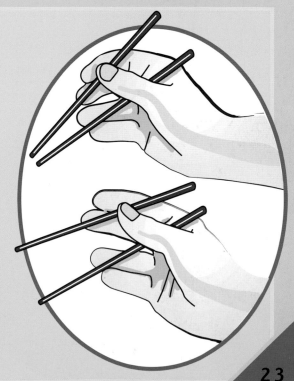

23

Salmon teriyaki

'Teriyaki' is the Japanese name for a sauce made from soy sauce and sugar. Teriyaki sauce can be eaten with many different ingredients, such as fish, chicken, tofu and vegetables. In this dish, it goes well with salmon.

What you need

1 tbsp sunflower oil
2 salmon steaks
100g mushrooms
50g bean sprouts
50ml soy sauce
1 tbsp granulated
  sugar

What you do

1 Cut the mushrooms into slices.

2 Put the soy sauce, sugar and 2 tbsp water into a saucepan. Bring the mixture to the **boil**, then **simmer** for about 10 minutes, stirring regularly, until the sauce is thick and syrupy.

3 Take the pan off the heat, and put a lid on it to keep the sauce warm.

(!) 4 Heat the oil in a frying pan, and add the sliced mushrooms and bean sprouts. **Fry** them for about 5 minutes, then put them into an ovenproof dish.

5 Turn the oven on to its lowest setting, and put the vegetables into the oven to keep warm.

6 Put the salmon steaks into the frying pan. Cook them for about 5 minutes on each side, until they are slightly brown and cooked through.

7 Put one salmon steak and some of the cooked vegetables onto each plate. Carefully spoon the sauce over the salmon.

Beef tataki

For this dish, the beef needs to **marinate** for at least 3 hours, so that it can soak up all the flavours of the sauce. Start making it well before you want to eat it!

What you need

225g steak
1 onion
½ tbsp lemon juice
50ml white wine
    vinegar (or malt
    vinegar)
50ml soy sauce
1 tbsp granulated
    sugar
lettuce leaves

What you do

1 Turn the grill on to a medium heat. **Grill** the steak for 15 minutes, turning halfway through so that both sides are cooked.

2 While the steak is cooking, **peel** the onion and finely **chop** half of it.

3 Cut the steak in half to check that it is cooked all the way through, not still red.

4 Mix together the chopped onion, lemon juice, white wine vinegar, soy sauce and sugar in a bowl. Add the steak, and coat it well with the **marinade**.

5 Leave the steak to marinate for at least 3 hours.

6 Remove the steak from the marinade. Cut it into thin **slices**.

7 Arrange the lettuce leaves on plates, and place the beef slices on top.

EATING MEAT

Meat is thought of as quite a luxury in Japan, as it is very expensive. It is usually cut into thin slices and served with vegetables or salad, as in this dish.

Steamed chicken
with broccoli

Most Japanese cooking is very healthy. This steamed chicken is particularly good for you, because it does not contain any fat.

What you need

2 chicken breasts
50ml soy sauce
½ tbsp granulated
    sugar
75g broccoli

What you do

1 Mix the soy sauce and sugar in a bowl. Put the chicken into the bowl, and leave to **marinate** for about an hour, turning once so that all the chicken is coated with the marinade.

(!) 2 Put the marinated chicken into a steamer over a saucepan of boiling water. Turn the heat down to low. **Steam** for 15 minutes, then turn the chicken over and steam for another 10 minutes.

3 Meanwhile, **chop** the broccoli into small pieces.

4 Bring a saucepan of water to the **boil**. Add the broccoli, and cook for 5 minutes.

(!) 5 Carefully take the chicken breasts out of the steamer using a fork to lift them. Put them onto a chopping board. Cut them into **slices** about 5mm thick.

6 Arrange the chicken slices and the broccoli on plates.

COOKING IN THE OVEN

If you don't have a steamer, you can cook the chicken in the oven. **Preheat** the oven to 200°C/400°F/gas mark 6. Put the chicken into an ovenproof dish. Half-fill a roasting tin with hot water, then carefully place the dish with the chicken in it into water. **Cover** the whole roasting tin with foil. Put the tin in the oven, and cook the chicken for 30 minutes.

Tuna and egg rice bowl

Japanese people eat a lot of fish and seafood. This tuna dish makes an ideal lunch or snack.

What you need

200g short grain rice
150g canned tuna
1 vegetable stock cube
1 onion
½ tbsp soy sauce
½ tbsp granulated sugar
1 egg

What you do

1 Put the rice into a colander. Put the colander under the cold tap, and run cold water through the rice until the water runs clear.

2 Put the rinsed rice into a saucepan, and add 400ml water. Put a lid on the pan. Bring the water to the **boil**, then lower the heat and **simmer** the rice for about 20 minutes, or until it has soaked up all the water.

3 Put the cooked rice into two small bowls.

4 **Drain** the tuna by emptying it into a colander or sieve and letting the liquid drain away.

5 Put the drained tuna into a bowl. Use a fork to break it up into small pieces.

6 Put 100ml water into a saucepan, and bring it to the boil. Crumble the stock cube into the water, and stir until it **dissolves**.

7 **Peel** and **chop** half the onion. Carefully add the chopped onion to the stock, and simmer for 5 minutes until the onion is soft.

8 Add the tuna, soy sauce and sugar to the stock. Simmer for 2 minutes.

⚠ 9 Spoon the stock from the pan over the bowls of rice (leaving the tuna and onions behind in the pan).

10 Crack the egg into a small bowl. **Beat** the egg with a fork or a whisk until the yolk and the white are mixed.

11 Pour the beaten egg over the tuna and onions. Put a lid on the pan, and cook for 3 minutes.

12 Spoon the tuna and egg mixture onto the rice, and serve.

Rice balls

Rice balls are the Japanese version of sandwiches. They are often put into packed lunches or taken on picnics. In this recipe, the rice balls are made in small bowls.

What you need

200g short grain rice
50g canned tuna
1 onion
½ tbsp granulated
  sugar
1 tbsp soy sauce

What you do

1 Put the rice into a colander. Put the colander under the cold tap, and run cold water through the rice until the water runs clear.

2 Put the rinsed rice into a saucepan, and add 400ml water. Put a lid on the pan. Bring the water to the **boil**, then lower the heat and **simmer** the rice for about 20 minutes, or until it has soaked up all the water.

3 **Drain** the tuna by emptying it into a colander or sieve and letting the liquid drain away.

4 Put the drained tuna into a bowl. Use a fork to break it up into small pieces.

5 **Peel** the skin from the onion and finely **chop** half of it.

6 Put the sugar, soy sauce and chopped onion into a saucepan.

7 Simmer the mixture until the sugar has **dissolved** and the onion is soft.

8 Add the tuna to the saucepan, and cook for a further 5 minutes.

9 Put 2 tbsp of the cooked rice into a small bowl. Make a hollow in the middle of the rice, and put 1 tsp of the tuna mixture into the hole. Then put another tsp of rice on top and shape the top into a ball with the spoon.

10 Repeat this process until you have used up all the rice and tuna mixture. You should have enough to fill four to six small bowls.

11 Leave the rice balls to **cool**. Serve them in the bowls, or lift them all out onto a large plate.

NORIMAKI

In Japan, rice is often wrapped in seaweed and rolled up. These rolls are called 'norimaki'. To make them, seaweed is grilled, the filling spooned onto it and the 'nori' rolled up into a tube. The tube is then sliced to make norimaki.

Grilled courgettes with ginger

This vegetable dish is simple to make. You could either serve it as a main course or as a side dish.

What you need

2 courgettes
½ vegetable stock cube
1 tbsp soy sauce
½ tbsp granulated
    sugar
2½ cm piece fresh
    ginger

What you do

1 With a sharp knife, cut the ends off the courgettes, then cut them in half lengthways.

2 Carefully **peel** the ginger using a sharp knife. Either **grate** or finely **chop** the ginger.

3 Arrange the courgette halves, skin side down, on a grill pan. **Grill** for 5 minutes, until they begin to brown.

4 Turn the courgette halves over, so the skin faces up. Grill for a further 5 minutes.

5 Put 50ml water into a saucepan, and bring it to the **boil**. Crumble half a stock cube into the water, and stir until it **dissolves**.

6 Add the soy sauce and sugar to the stock, and **simmer** for 5 minutes.

7 Arrange the courgette halves onto plates, then pour the sauce over them.

8 Sprinkle the grated or chopped ginger over the courgettes, then serve.

AUBERGINE ALTERNATIVE

You could try making this dish with aubergines instead of courgettes. Cut the aubergines into slices, then grill them for 10 minutes on each side.

Sweet potatoes with soy sauce

This side dish will go well with most of the main courses in this book, especially steamed chicken with broccoli (see page 28), beef tataki (see page 26) and salmon teriyaki (see page 24).

What you need

2 sweet potatoes
75g granulated sugar
2 tbsp soy sauce

What you do

1 **Peel** the skin from the sweet potatoes, then cut them into **slices** about 2cm thick.

2 Put the slices of sweet potato into a saucepan. Add enough water to nearly cover them.

3 Add the sugar, and **cover** the pan.

4 Bring the water to the **boil**, then **simmer** for about 15 minutes, until the potatoes are soft.

⃠ 5 **Drain** the water from the potatoes, then sprinkle them with the soy sauce before serving.

YAKI-IMO!

In Japan, baked sweet potatoes, known as 'yaki-imo', are often sold in the street. They are baked over fires or on hot stones, and are particularly popular during the cold Japanese winters. The yaki-imo seller pushes a cart through the streets, calling out 'Yaki-imo!' to attract customers.

Green beans with sesame seeds

Sesame seeds are often used as part of a dressing or sauce in Japanese cooking. They go very well with the beans in this recipe.

What you need

100g green beans
1 tbsp sesame seeds
½ tbsp granulated
   sugar
½ tbsp soy sauce

What you do

1 Cut the stalk ends off the green beans, then cut them into 5cm long pieces.

(!) 2 Fill a saucepan with water, and bring it to the **boil**. Add the beans, and cook for 2 minutes. **Drain** the beans, and put them into a large bowl.

(!) 3 Put the sesame seeds into a frying pan without adding any oil. **Toast** them over a medium heat for about 5 minutes, tossing them occasionally, until they are golden brown. Beware of seeds popping out!

4 Mix the toasted sesame seeds, sugar, soy sauce and ½ tbsp water in a small bowl.

5 Pour the dressing over the beans, and serve.

CABBAGE LEAVES

This sesame seed dressing could be used to dress
other vegetables. Try cooking some Chinese cabbage leaves
by carefully lowering them into boiling water for about
a minute, draining them, then pouring the sesame seed
dressing over them.

Toffee sweet potatoes

What you need

225g sweet potatoes
75g granulated sugar
1 tbsp sesame seeds

Traditional Japanese food does not include many desserts. However, Japanese people sometimes eat cakes and other sweet dishes as a snack with a cup of tea (see page 41).

What you do

1 **Peel** the skin from the sweet potatoes, and cut them into **slices** about 1½ cm thick.

(!) 2 Put the sesame seeds into a frying pan without adding any oil. **Toast** them over a medium heat for about 5 minutes, tossing them occasionally, until they are golden brown. Put the toasted sesame seeds to one side.

3 Put the slices of sweet potato into a saucepan, and cover them with water.

4 Bring the water to the **boil**, then **simmer** the potatoes for 10 minutes, until they are just beginning to go soft.

(!) 5 **Drain** the potatoes, and put them on one side.

(!) 6 Put the sugar into a pan with 50ml water, and bring the mixture to the boil. Boil it for about 7 minutes, without stirring, until the mixture turns into a light brown syrup.

(!) **7** Add the cooked sweet potato slices to the warm syrup, turning them so that they are well coated. Sprinkle them with the toasted sesame seeds.

8 Put a sheet of greaseproof paper onto a plate. Take the potatoes out of the pan, one by one, and lay them on the paper.

9 Leave the potatoes until the toffee syrup hardens.

GREEN TEA

Japanese people drink green tea with everything! Green tea is drunk plain, without milk or sugar. You should be able to find green tea in your local supermarket or delicatessen – why not try drinking it with the recipes in this book?

Japanese lunch box

Lunch boxes, known as 'bento', are very common in Japan. People take lunch boxes to work or school, but they are also sold in railway stations, theatres and restaurants.

You can put any sort of food into your lunch box, although it is probably not a very good idea to include clear soup! Lunch boxes are a good way of using up any leftovers from your Japanese cooking. Here are some of the recipes in this book you could use:

- grilled tofu (see page 14)
- grilled chicken (see page 16)
- salmon teriyaki (see page 24)
- beef tataki (see page 26)
- steamed chicken with broccoli (see page 28)
- sweet potatoes with soy sauce (see page 36)
- green beans with sesame seeds (see page 38)
- rice balls (see page 32)
- toffee sweet potatoes (see page 40)

Some Japanese lunch boxes also include fresh fruit.

ROLLED OMELETTE

Here is a quick and easy recipe that's ideal to go in a lunch box. Make one omelette for each person.

What you need

2 eggs
1 tbsp soy sauce
½ tsp granulated
   sugar
½ tbsp sunflower oil

What you do

1 Crack the eggs into a small bowl. **Beat** them with a fork or whisk until the yolk and the white are mixed. Add the soy sauce and sugar, and mix well.

(!)2 Heat the oil in a frying pan over a medium heat. Pour in the egg, and tilt the pan so that the mixture spreads evenly over the bottom of the pan.

3 Cook the omelette for about 5 minutes, until it is set.

4 Tip the omelette onto a chopping board. Wait for it to cool for a minute or two. Roll the omelette up into a tube-shape, and leave it to cool for at least 5 more minutes.

5 When it is cool, cut the omelette into **slices** about 2cm thick.

43

Further information

Here are some places to find out more about Japan and Japanese cooking.

Books

A Taste of Japan
Jenny Ridgewell, Thomson Learning, 1993
Food in Japan
Jiro Takeshita, The Rourke Book Company, 1989
Cooking the Japanese Way
Reiko Weston, Lerner Publications Company, 1989
Next Stop: Japan
Fred Martin, Heinemann Library, 1998

Websites

soar.berkeley.edu/recipes/ethnic/japanese
www.astray.com/recipes/?search=japanese
www.yumyum.com/recipes.html
www.jinjapan.org/kidsweb/japan/word.html

Conversion chart

Ingredients for recipes can be measured in two different ways. Metric measurements use grams and millilitres. Imperial measurements use ounces and fluid ounces. This book uses metric measurements. The chart here shows you how to convert measurements from metric to imperial.

SOLIDS		LIQUIDS	
METRIC	IMPERIAL	METRIC	IMPERIAL
10g	¼ oz	30ml	1 fl oz
15g	½ oz	50ml	2 fl oz
25g	1 oz	75ml	2½ fl oz
50g	1¾ oz	100ml	3½ fl oz
75g	2¾ oz	125ml	4 fl oz
100g	3½ oz	150ml	5 fl oz
150g	5 oz	300ml	10 fl oz
250g	9 oz	600ml	20 fl oz

Healthy eating

This diagram shows which foods you should eat to stay healthy. Most of your food should come from the bottom of the pyramid. Eat some of the foods from the middle every day. Only eat a little of the foods from the top.

Healthy eating, Japanese style!

Japanese food includes lots of rice and noodles, which belong to the bottom layer of the pyramid. Japanese people also eat a lot of vegetables, some fish, and a little meat. They eat very few desserts, so you can see how healthy Japanese cooking is!

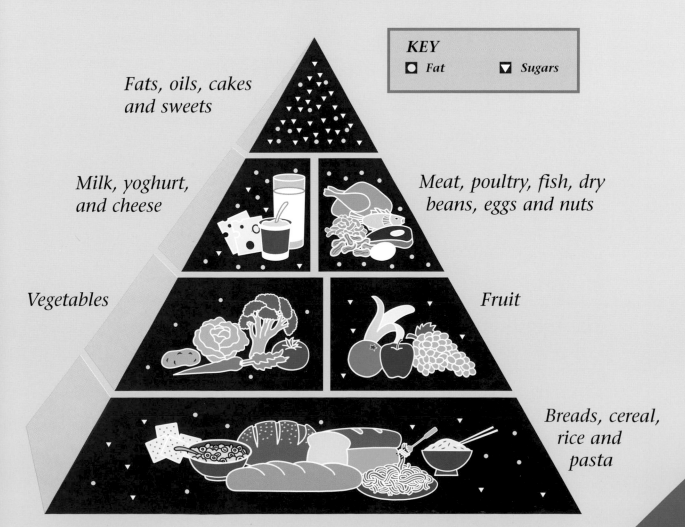

KEY
◻ Fat   ▽ Sugars

Fats, oils, cakes and sweets

Milk, yoghurt, and cheese

Meat, poultry, fish, dry beans, eggs and nuts

Vegetables

Fruit

Breads, cereal, rice and pasta

Glossary

beat mix something together strongly, for example egg yolks and whites

boil cook a liquid on the hob. Boiling liquid bubbles and steams strongly.

chop cut something into pieces using a knife

cool allow hot food to become cold. Always let food cool down before putting it in the fridge.

cover put a lid on a pan, or foil over a dish

dissolve mix something until it disappears into a liquid

drain remove water, usually by pouring something into a colander or sieve

fry cook something in oil in a pan

grate break something, for example cheese, into tiny pieces using a grater

grill cook something under the grill

humid a climate that is hot and wet

isolated cut off from other people or the rest of the world

marinate soak something, for example meat or fish, in a mixture called the **marinade** before cooking, so that it absorbs the taste of the mixture

peel remove the skin of a fruit or vegetable

preheat turn on the oven in advance, so that it is hot when you are ready to use it

pulp a mixture that has been mashed until smooth

simmer cook a liquid gently on the hob. Simmering liquid bubbles and steams gently.

slice cut something into thin, flat pieces

steam cook something in the steam from boiling water

stir-fry frying over a high heat, stirring the food all the time

toasted heated in a pan without any oil

vegetarian food that does not contain meat, or fish. People who don't eat meat or fish are called vegetarians.

Index